THE AUTO SALES

L O G   B O O K

Keep Track of Your Sales, Clients and
Most Importantly....Your Money!

Written by Evan Henry

If found, please return to

Name:

_____

Phone:

_____

Email:

_____

Reward:

_____

GREEN PEA OR VETERAN:

Why do you sell cars? Is it for fun? I'd hope not. Is it because you genuinely enjoy cars? Maybe, in the beginning. The real answer is you want to make money. This can be a lucrative career, if you succeed. **YOU** need to track and monitor every car you sell. The importance of this cannot be overstated. Why sell a car if you're not getting paid for it? Tracking your deals means you're tracking your money! Use this book to log and keep notes on every single deal you close. I don't care if you're 18 or 80. The beauty of this book is that it works for all brands, dealerships, and especially used car lots. From Jet Ski's to John Deere, it doesn't matter what you're selling. Whatever unit you move, you need to be able to track it. Within this book you'll find 200 deal sheets, a "VIP list", a "Looking For" file, and a lot more. If you sell over 200 units in one year, buy a second book. You can afford it.

Don't worry about the dealership changing the CRM on you anymore. Just think of how many repeat clients of yours could be mistakenly reassigned, orphaned, or even worse, forgotten about entirely. I've lived it and I've lost clients over it. It is statistically proven that you will make more gross on **YOUR** repeat clients than a fresh up. You already have their **TRUST**, now keep it!

You **CANNOT** rely on Management and your back office to get you paid. How can you be okay with letting someone with no skin in the game control your income? I know the majority of your associates work hard and won't actively try to screw you over. I'm positive of that. However, I'm also positive that mistakes happen. Do you really want to miss a bonus unit because you didn't keep track of your deals? That could cost you hundreds or even thousands of dollars! As a matter of fact, during the writing of this book, I learned a friend of mine miscounted his deals and decided to sandbag a deal for the next month. Panic set in about two hours before close of business on the last day of the month. It cost him **THOUSANDS** of dollars. This is not an exaggeration. I saw this happen. Guess who's buying the first copy? Well, not him.

He can't afford it.

One day you're going to consider moving stores. Hell, you probably already are. Whether it's for a shorter commute, better inventory, or maybe move to a family owned store, it will happen. Let alone the possibility of you getting fired. It probably wouldn't hurt to have your book of business along for your next interview. You could try your hand at five different dealerships before you find the right fit. With this book and a couple of minutes logging each deal, you'll have your own portable CRM that nobody can take away.

Provide exceptional service by using the "Notes" tab not just to draw on, but to remember the important information about the car you sold, traded, or the client themselves. Did you hold a grand on the trade? Better make a note of it and check that ACV later. These pages will provide you with space for all the information you want and need to keep.

Fill it out completely, or don't. Spend two minutes writing down what you feel is important. Don't get hung up on filling out every detail. Log the information **YOU** feel is important to **YOU**!

THE ROAD TO THE SALE

1. Meet and Greet

2. Needs Assessment

3. Vehicle Selection

4. Walk-Around

5. Demo Drive

6. Trade Evaluation

7. Present Numbers and Ask for the Sale

8. Close

9. F&I

10. Delivery and Service Introduction

QUICK REFERENCE WORK EXTENSIONS

NAME	DEPARTMENT	EXTENSION

MAKE CALLING VIN NUMBERS A LITTLE EASIER

A - Alpha	N - November
B - Bravo	O - Oscar
C - Charlie	P - Papa
D - Delta	Q - Quebec
E - Echo	R - Romeo
F - Foxtrot	S - Sierra
G - Golf	T - Tango
H - Hotel	U - Uniform
I - India	V - Victor
J - Juliett	W - Whiskey
K - Kilo	X - X-Ray
L - Lima	Y - Yankee
M - Mike	Z - Zulu

PASSWORDS

(You're guaranteed to forget them.)

Website:	
Username:	
Password:	

Website:	
Username:	
Password:	

Website:	
Username:	
Password:	

Website:	
Username:	
Password:	

Website:	
Username:	
Password:	

Website:	
Username:	
Password:	

Website:	
Username:	
Password:	

Website:	
Username:	
Password:	

Website:	
Username:	
Password:	

Website:	
Username:	
Password:	

PASSWORDS

(You're guaranteed to forget them.)

Website:	
Username:	
Password:	
Website:	
Username:	
Password:	
Website:	
Username:	
Password:	
Website:	
Username:	
Password:	
Website:	
Username:	
Password:	
Website:	
Username:	
Password:	
Website:	
Username:	
Password:	
Website:	
Username:	
Password:	
Website:	
Username:	
Password:	
Website:	
Username:	
Password:	

ON THE LOOKOUT!

Name	Car	Details

ON THE LOOKOUT!

Name	Car	Details

VIP CLIENTS

Name:	
Phone:	
Email:	
Notes:	

Name:	
Phone:	
Email:	
Notes:	

Name:	
Phone:	
Email:	
Notes:	

VIP CLIENTS

Name:	
Phone:	
Email:	
Notes:	

Name:	
Phone:	
Email:	
Notes:	

Name:	
Phone:	
Email:	
Notes:	

VIP CLIENTS

Name:	
Phone:	
Email:	
Notes:	

Name:	
Phone:	
Email:	
Notes:	

Name:	
Phone:	
Email:	
Notes:	

VIP CLIENTS

Name:	
Phone:	
Email:	
Notes:	

Name:	
Phone:	
Email:	
Notes:	

Name:	
Phone:	
Email:	
Notes:	

Now, put this book
down, slam a Redbull,
and GO CATCH AN UP!

PRO TIP

Use the box in the upper right-hand corner to log which month the deal is counted. This is a quick way to sort through your year as each month will have a different number of deals logged. See this example:

<u>Feb</u> /2019

New ✓ CPO ☐ Used ☐   Date <u>03/17/2006</u>

Deal Number: <u>22562</u>   Stock Number: <u>H175623</u>

Client's Name: <u>Bernard Jones</u>

Spouse: <u>Shirley</u>

Make: <u>Ford</u>   Model: <u>F-150 King Ranch</u>

Trade Yes/No   Trade Stock # <u>H175624</u>

Make: <u>Toyota</u>   Model: <u>Tundra</u>

Repeat/Referral: Y/N _____

NOTES:

Goes by Ned. Nice couple from Des Moines. Had to over allow $1,000 and throw in two key chains. Put receipt in folder to claim on taxes.

_____
_____
_____
_____

New ☐ CPO ☐ Used ☐   Date ___/___/___

Deal Number: _____ Stock Number: _____

Client's Name: _____/Spouse: _____

Make: _____ Model: _____

Trade Yes/No   Trade Stock # _____

Make: _____ Model: _____

Repeat/Referral: Y/N _____

NOTES:

_____

_____

_____

_____

_____

_____

_____

_____

_____

_____

_____

_____

_____/20_____

New ☐ CPO ☐ Used ☐   Date ___/___/_____

Deal Number: _____ Stock Number: _____

Client's Name: _____/Spouse: _____

Make: _____ Model: _____

Trade Yes/No   Trade Stock # _____

Make: _____ Model: _____

Repeat/Referral: Y/N _____

NOTES:

_____
_____
_____
_____
_____
_____
_____
_____
_____
_____
_____
_____
_____

New ☐ CPO ☐ Used ☐   Date ___/___/___

Deal Number: _____ Stock Number: _____

Client's Name: _____/Spouse: _____

Make: _____ Model: _____

Trade Yes/No   Trade Stock # _____

Make: _____ Model: _____

Repeat/Referral: Y/N _____

NOTES:

_____

_____

_____

_____

_____

_____

_____

_____

_____

_____

_____

_____

_____ /20 _____

New ☐ CPO ☐ Used ☐   Date ___/___/_____

Deal Number: _____ Stock Number: _____

Client's Name: _____/Spouse: _____

Make: _____ Model: _____

Trade Yes/No   Trade Stock # _____

Make: _____ Model: _____

Repeat/Referral: Y/N _____

NOTES:

_____
_____
_____
_____
_____
_____
_____
_____
_____
_____
_____
_____
_____
_____

New ☐ CPO ☐ Used ☐   Date ___ / ___ / ___

Deal Number: _____ Stock Number: _____

Client's Name: _____ /Spouse: _____

Make: _____ Model: _____

Trade Yes/No   Trade Stock # _____

Make: _____ Model: _____

Repeat/Referral: Y/N _____

NOTES:

_____

_____

_____

_____

_____

_____

_____

_____

_____

_____

_____

_____

New ☐ CPO ☐ Used ☐   Date ___/___/_____

Deal Number: _____ Stock Number: _____

Client's Name: _____/Spouse: _____

Make: _____ Model: _____

Trade Yes/No   Trade Stock # _____

Make: _____ Model: _____

Repeat/Referral: Y/N _____

NOTES:

_____
_____
_____
_____
_____
_____
_____
_____
_____
_____
_____
_____
_____

_____ /20

New ☐ CPO ☐ Used ☐   Date ___/___/___

Deal Number: _____ Stock Number: _____

Client's Name: _____/Spouse: _____

Make: _____ Model: _____

Trade Yes/No   Trade Stock # _____

Make: _____ Model: _____

Repeat/Referral: Y/N _____

NOTES:

_____

_____

_____

_____

_____

_____

_____

_____

_____

_____

_____

_____

New ☐ CPO ☐ Used ☐   Date ___/___/___

Deal Number: _____ Stock Number: _____

Client's Name: _____/Spouse: _____

Make: _____ Model: _____

Trade Yes/No   Trade Stock # _____

Make: _____ Model: _____

Repeat/Referral: Y/N _____

NOTES:

_____

_____

_____

_____

_____

_____

_____

_____

_____

_____

_____

_____

New ☐ CPO ☐ Used ☐   Date ___/___/___

Deal Number: _____ Stock Number: _____

Client's Name: _____/Spouse: _____

Make: _____ Model: _____

Trade Yes/No   Trade Stock # _____

Make: _____ Model: _____

Repeat/Referral: Y/N _____

NOTES:

_____

_____

_____

_____

_____

_____

_____

_____

_____

_____

_____

New ☐ CPO ☐ Used ☐   Date ___/___/_____

Deal Number: _____ Stock Number: _____

Client's Name: _____/Spouse: _____

Make: _____ Model: _____

Trade Yes/No   Trade Stock # _____

Make: _____ Model: _____

Repeat/Referral: Y/N _____

NOTES:

_____

_____

_____

_____

_____

_____

_____

_____

_____

_____

_____

_____

New ☐ CPO ☐ Used ☐   Date __/__/__

Deal Number: _____ Stock Number: _____

Client's Name: _____/Spouse: _____

Make: _____   Model: _____

Trade Yes/No   Trade Stock # _____

Make: _____   Model: _____

Repeat/Referral: Y/N _____

NOTES:

_____
_____
_____
_____
_____
_____
_____
_____
_____
_____
_____

_____ /20

New ☐ CPO ☐ Used ☐   Date ___/___/___

Deal Number: _____ Stock Number: _____

Client's Name: _____/Spouse: _____

Make: _____ Model: _____

Trade Yes/No   Trade Stock # _____

Make: _____ Model: _____

Repeat/Referral: Y/N _____

NOTES:

_____

_____

_____

_____

_____

_____

_____

_____

_____

_____

_____

_____

_____ /20

New ☐ CPO ☐ Used ☐   Date ___/___/___

Deal Number: _____ Stock Number: _____

Client's Name: _____/Spouse: _____

Make: _____ Model: _____

Trade Yes/No   Trade Stock # _____

Make: _____ Model: _____

Repeat/Referral: Y/N _____

NOTES:

_____

_____

_____

_____

_____

_____

_____

_____

_____

_____

_____

_____ /20

New ☐ CPO ☐ Used ☐   Date ___/___/___

Deal Number: _____ Stock Number: _____

Client's Name: _____/Spouse: _____

Make: _____ Model: _____

Trade Yes/No   Trade Stock # _____

Make: _____ Model: _____

Repeat/Referral: Y/N _____

NOTES:

_____

_____

_____

_____

_____

_____

_____

_____

_____

_____

_____

_____

New ☐ CPO ☐ Used ☐   Date __/__/__

Deal Number: _____ Stock Number: _____

Client's Name: _____/Spouse: _____

Make: _____ Model: _____

Trade Yes/No   Trade Stock # _____

Make: _____ Model: _____

Repeat/Referral: Y/N _____

NOTES:

_____

_____

_____

_____

_____

_____

_____

_____

_____

_____

_____

_____

_____/20

New ☐ CPO ☐ Used ☐   Date ___/___/___

Deal Number: _____ Stock Number: _____

Client's Name: _____/Spouse: _____

Make: _____ Model: _____

Trade Yes/No   Trade Stock # _____

Make: _____ Model: _____

Repeat/Referral: Y/N _____

NOTES:

_____

_____

_____

_____

_____

_____

_____

_____

_____

_____

_____

_____

_____

_____ /20

New ☐ CPO ☐ Used ☐   Date ___/___/___

Deal Number: _____ Stock Number: _____

Client's Name: _____/Spouse: _____

Make: _____ Model: _____

Trade Yes/No   Trade Stock # _____

Make: _____ Model: _____

Repeat/Referral: Y/N _____

NOTES:

_____

_____

_____

_____

_____

_____

_____

_____

_____

_____

_____

_____

_____ /20

New ☐ CPO ☐ Used ☐   Date ___/___/___

Deal Number: _____ Stock Number: _____

Client's Name: _____/Spouse: _____

Make: _____ Model: _____

Trade Yes/No   Trade Stock # _____

Make: _____ Model: _____

Repeat/Referral: Y/N _____

NOTES:

_____
_____
_____
_____
_____
_____
_____
_____
_____
_____
_____
_____

_____/20_____

New ☐ CPO ☐ Used ☐   Date ___/___/_____

Deal Number: _____ Stock Number: _____

Client's Name: _____/Spouse: _____

Make: _____ Model: _____

Trade Yes/No   Trade Stock # _____

Make: _____ Model: _____

Repeat/Referral: Y/N _____

NOTES:

_____

_____

_____

_____

_____

_____

_____

_____

_____

_____

_____

_____

_____/20

New ☐ CPO ☐ Used ☐   Date ___/___/___

Deal Number: _____ Stock Number: _____

Client's Name: _____/Spouse: _____

Make: _____ Model: _____

Trade Yes/No   Trade Stock # _____

Make: _____ Model: _____

Repeat/Referral: Y/N _____

NOTES:

_____
_____
_____
_____
_____
_____
_____
_____
_____
_____
_____
_____
_____

New ☐ CPO ☐ Used ☐   Date ___/___/___

Deal Number: _____ Stock Number: _____

Client's Name: _____/Spouse: _____

Make: _____   Model: _____

Trade Yes/No   Trade Stock # _____

Make: _____   Model: _____

Repeat/Referral: Y/N _____

NOTES:

_____
_____
_____
_____
_____
_____
_____
_____
_____
_____
_____
_____

_____/20

New ☐ CPO ☐ Used ☐   Date ___/___/___

Deal Number: _____ Stock Number: _____

Client's Name: _____/Spouse: _____

Make: _____ Model: _____

Trade Yes/No   Trade Stock # _____

Make: _____ Model: _____

Repeat/Referral: Y/N _____

NOTES:

_____
_____
_____
_____
_____
_____
_____
_____
_____
_____
_____
_____

New ☐ CPO ☐ Used ☐   Date ___/___/___

Deal Number: _____ Stock Number: _____

Client's Name: _____/Spouse: _____

Make: _____   Model: _____

Trade Yes/No   Trade Stock # _____

Make: _____   Model: _____

Repeat/Referral: Y/N _____

NOTES:

_____

_____

_____

_____

_____

_____

_____

_____

_____

_____

_____

_____

_____

New ☐ CPO ☐ Used ☐   Date ___/___/___

Deal Number: _____ Stock Number: _____

Client's Name: _____/Spouse: _____

Make: _____ Model: _____

Trade Yes/No   Trade Stock # _____

Make: _____ Model: _____

Repeat/Referral: Y/N _____

NOTES:

_____

_____

_____

_____

_____

_____

_____

_____

_____

_____

_____

_____

New ☐ CPO ☐ Used ☐   Date __ / __ / ____

Deal Number: _____ Stock Number: _____

Client's Name: _____/Spouse: _____

Make: _____ Model: _____

Trade Yes/No   Trade Stock # _____

Make: _____ Model: _____

Repeat/Referral: Y/N _____

NOTES:

_____

_____

_____

_____

_____

_____

_____

_____

_____

_____

_____

_____

New ☐ CPO ☐ Used ☐   Date ___/___/___

Deal Number: _____ Stock Number: _____

Client's Name: _____/Spouse: _____

Make: _____ Model: _____

Trade Yes/No   Trade Stock # _____

Make: _____ Model: _____

Repeat/Referral: Y/N _____

NOTES:

_____

_____

_____

_____

_____

_____

_____

_____

_____

_____

_____

_____

New ☐ CPO ☐ Used ☐   Date __/__/____

Deal Number: _____ Stock Number: _____

Client's Name: _____/Spouse: _____

Make: _____ Model: _____

Trade Yes/No   Trade Stock # _____

Make: _____ Model: _____

Repeat/Referral: Y/N _____

NOTES:

_____
_____
_____
_____
_____
_____
_____
_____
_____
_____
_____
_____

New ☐ CPO ☐ Used ☐   Date ___/___/___

Deal Number: _____ Stock Number: _____

Client's Name: _____/Spouse: _____

Make: _____ Model: _____

Trade Yes/No   Trade Stock # _____

Make: _____ Model: _____

Repeat/Referral: Y/N _____

NOTES:

_____

_____

_____

_____

_____

_____

_____

_____

_____

_____

_____

New ☐ CPO ☐ Used ☐   Date __/__/____

Deal Number: _____ Stock Number: _____

Client's Name: _____/Spouse: _____

Make: _____ Model: _____

Trade Yes/No   Trade Stock # _____

Make: _____ Model: _____

Repeat/Referral: Y/N _____

NOTES:

_____

_____

_____

_____

_____

_____

_____

_____

_____

_____

_____

_____

_____ /20 _____

New ☐ CPO ☐ Used ☐   Date ___/___/_____

Deal Number: _____ Stock Number: _____

Client's Name: _____/Spouse: _____

Make: _____ Model: _____

Trade Yes/No   Trade Stock # _____

Make: _____ Model: _____

Repeat/Referral: Y/N _____

NOTES:

_____

_____

_____

_____

_____

_____

_____

_____

_____

_____

_____

_____

New ☐ CPO ☐ Used ☐   Date __/__/____

Deal Number: _____ Stock Number: _____

Client's Name: _____/Spouse: _____

Make: _____ Model: _____

Trade Yes/No   Trade Stock # _____

Make: _____ Model: _____

Repeat/Referral: Y/N _____

NOTES:

_____
_____
_____
_____
_____
_____
_____
_____
_____
_____
_____
_____

New ☐ CPO ☐ Used ☐   Date ___/___/___

Deal Number: _____ Stock Number: _____

Client's Name: _____/Spouse: _____

Make: _____ Model: _____

Trade Yes/No   Trade Stock # _____

Make: _____ Model: _____

Repeat/Referral: Y/N _____

NOTES:

_____

_____

_____

_____

_____

_____

_____

_____

_____

_____

_____

_____ /20 _____

New ☐ CPO ☐ Used ☐   Date __/__/____

Deal Number: _____ Stock Number: _____

Client's Name: _____/Spouse: _____

Make: _____ Model: _____

Trade Yes/No   Trade Stock # _____

Make: _____ Model: _____

Repeat/Referral: Y/N _____

NOTES:

_____

_____

_____

_____

_____

_____

_____

_____

_____

_____

_____

_____

_____

New ☐ CPO ☐ Used ☐   Date ___ / ___ / ___

Deal Number: _____ Stock Number: _____

Client's Name: _____ /Spouse: _____

Make: _____ Model: _____

Trade Yes/No   Trade Stock # _____

Make: _____ Model: _____

Repeat/Referral: Y/N _____

NOTES:

_____

_____

_____

_____

_____

_____

_____

_____

_____

_____

_____

_____

_____

_____ /20

New ☐ CPO ☐ Used ☐   Date __/__/__

Deal Number: _____ Stock Number: _____

Client's Name: _____/Spouse: _____

Make: _____ Model: _____

Trade Yes/No   Trade Stock # _____

Make: _____ Model: _____

Repeat/Referral: Y/N _____

NOTES:

_____

_____

_____

_____

_____

_____

_____

_____

_____

_____

_____

_____

_____

_____ /20

New ☐ CPO ☐ Used ☐   Date ___/___/___

Deal Number: _____ Stock Number: _____

Client's Name: _____/Spouse: _____

Make: _____ Model: _____

Trade Yes/No   Trade Stock # _____

Make: _____ Model: _____

Repeat/Referral: Y/N _____

NOTES:

_____

_____

_____

_____

_____

_____

_____

_____

_____

_____

_____

_____

New ☐ CPO ☐ Used ☐   Date ___/___/___

Deal Number: _____ Stock Number: _____

Client's Name: _____/Spouse: _____

Make: _____ Model: _____

Trade Yes/No   Trade Stock # _____

Make: _____ Model: _____

Repeat/Referral: Y/N _____

NOTES:

_____
_____
_____
_____
_____
_____
_____
_____
_____
_____
_____
_____

New ☐ CPO ☐ Used ☐   Date ___/___/___

Deal Number: _____ Stock Number: _____

Client's Name: _____/Spouse: _____

Make: _____ Model: _____

Trade Yes/No   Trade Stock # _____

Make: _____ Model: _____

Repeat/Referral: Y/N _____

NOTES:

_____

_____

_____

_____

_____

_____

_____

_____

_____

_____

_____

_____

_____ /20 _____

New ☐ CPO ☐ Used ☐   Date __/__/____

Deal Number: _____ Stock Number: _____

Client's Name: _____/Spouse: _____

Make: _____ Model: _____

Trade Yes/No   Trade Stock # _____

Make: _____ Model: _____

Repeat/Referral: Y/N _____

NOTES:

_____
_____
_____
_____
_____
_____
_____
_____
_____
_____
_____
_____

_____ /20

New ☐ CPO ☐ Used ☐   Date ___/___/___

Deal Number: _____ Stock Number: _____

Client's Name: _____/Spouse: _____

Make: _____ Model: _____

Trade Yes/No   Trade Stock # _____

Make: _____ Model: _____

Repeat/Referral: Y/N _____

NOTES:

_____
_____
_____
_____
_____
_____
_____
_____
_____
_____
_____
_____

New ☐ CPO ☐ Used ☐   Date ___/___/___

Deal Number: _____ Stock Number: _____

Client's Name: _____/Spouse: _____

Make: _____ Model: _____

Trade Yes/No   Trade Stock # _____

Make: _____ Model: _____

Repeat/Referral: Y/N _____

NOTES:

_____

_____

_____

_____

_____

_____

_____

_____

_____

_____

_____

_____

_____

_____ /20 _____

New ☐ CPO ☐ Used ☐   Date ___/___/___

Deal Number: _____ Stock Number: _____

Client's Name: _____/Spouse: _____

Make: _____ Model: _____

Trade Yes/No   Trade Stock # _____

Make: _____ Model: _____

Repeat/Referral: Y/N _____

NOTES:

_____
_____
_____
_____
_____
_____
_____
_____
_____
_____
_____
_____
_____

New ☐ CPO ☐ Used ☐   Date ___ / ___ / ___

Deal Number: _____ Stock Number: _____

Client's Name: _____/Spouse: _____

Make: _____ Model: _____

Trade Yes/No   Trade Stock # _____

Make: _____ Model: _____

Repeat/Referral: Y/N _____

NOTES:

_____

_____

_____

_____

_____

_____

_____

_____

_____

_____

_____

_____

New ☐ CPO ☐ Used ☐   Date ___/___/___

Deal Number: _____ Stock Number: _____

Client's Name: _____/Spouse: _____

Make: _____ Model: _____

Trade Yes/No   Trade Stock # _____

Make: _____ Model: _____

Repeat/Referral: Y/N _____

NOTES:

_____

_____

_____

_____

_____

_____

_____

_____

_____

_____

_____

_____

_____

New ☐ CPO ☐ Used ☐   Date ___/___/___

Deal Number: _____ Stock Number: _____

Client's Name: _____/Spouse: _____

Make: _____ Model: _____

Trade Yes/No   Trade Stock # _____

Make: _____ Model: _____

Repeat/Referral: Y/N _____

NOTES:

_____

_____

_____

_____

_____

_____

_____

_____

_____

_____

_____

_____

_____

_____ /20

New ☐ CPO ☐ Used ☐   Date ___/___/___

Deal Number: _____ Stock Number: _____

Client's Name: _____/Spouse: _____

Make: _____ Model: _____

Trade Yes/No   Trade Stock # _____

Make: _____ Model: _____

Repeat/Referral: Y/N _____

NOTES:

_____

_____

_____

_____

_____

_____

_____

_____

_____

_____

_____

_____

_____ /20

New ☐ CPO ☐ Used ☐   Date ___ / ___ / ___

Deal Number: _____ Stock Number: _____

Client's Name: _____/Spouse: _____

Make: _____ Model: _____

Trade Yes/No   Trade Stock # _____

Make: _____ Model: _____

Repeat/Referral: Y/N _____

NOTES:

_____
_____
_____
_____
_____
_____
_____
_____
_____
_____
_____
_____
_____

New ☐ CPO ☐ Used ☐   Date ___/___/___

Deal Number: _____ Stock Number: _____

Client's Name: _____/Spouse: _____

Make: _____ Model: _____

Trade Yes/No   Trade Stock # _____

Make: _____ Model: _____

Repeat/Referral: Y/N _____

NOTES:

_____

_____

_____

_____

_____

_____

_____

_____

_____

_____

_____

_____

_____ /20

New ☐ CPO ☐ Used ☐   Date ___/___/___

Deal Number: _____ Stock Number: _____

Client's Name: _____/Spouse: _____

Make: _____ Model: _____

Trade Yes/No   Trade Stock # _____

Make: _____ Model: _____

Repeat/Referral: Y/N _____

NOTES:

_____
_____
_____
_____
_____
_____
_____
_____
_____
_____
_____
_____

New ☐ CPO ☐ Used ☐   Date ___/___/___

Deal Number: _____ Stock Number: _____

Client's Name: _____/Spouse: _____

Make: _____ Model: _____

Trade Yes/No   Trade Stock # _____

Make: _____ Model: _____

Repeat/Referral: Y/N _____

NOTES:

_____

_____

_____

_____

_____

_____

_____

_____

_____

_____

_____

_____

_____ /20

New ☐ CPO ☐ Used ☐   Date __/__/____

Deal Number: _____ Stock Number: _____

Client's Name: _____/Spouse: _____

Make: _____ Model: _____

Trade Yes/No   Trade Stock # _____

Make: _____ Model: _____

Repeat/Referral: Y/N _____

NOTES:

_____
_____
_____
_____
_____
_____
_____
_____
_____
_____
_____
_____

_____ /20 _____

New ☐ CPO ☐ Used ☐   Date ___/___/___

Deal Number: _____ Stock Number: _____

Client's Name: _____/Spouse: _____

Make: _____ Model: _____

Trade Yes/No   Trade Stock # _____

Make: _____ Model: _____

Repeat/Referral: Y/N _____

NOTES:

_____

_____

_____

_____

_____

_____

_____

_____

_____

_____

_____

_____

_____/20

New ☐ CPO ☐ Used ☐   Date ___/___/___

Deal Number: _____ Stock Number: _____

Client's Name: _____/Spouse: _____

Make: _____ Model: _____

Trade Yes/No   Trade Stock # _____

Make: _____ Model: _____

Repeat/Referral: Y/N _____

NOTES:

_____
_____
_____
_____
_____
_____
_____
_____
_____
_____
_____
_____
_____

_____ /20 _____

New ☐ CPO ☐ Used ☐   Date ___/___/___

Deal Number: _____ Stock Number: _____

Client's Name: _____/Spouse: _____

Make: _____ Model: _____

Trade Yes/No   Trade Stock # _____

Make: _____ Model: _____

Repeat/Referral: Y/N _____

NOTES:

_____
_____
_____
_____
_____
_____
_____
_____
_____
_____
_____
_____

_____ /20

New ☐ CPO ☐ Used ☐   Date __/__/__

Deal Number: _____ Stock Number: _____

Client's Name: _____/Spouse: _____

Make: _____ Model: _____

Trade Yes/No   Trade Stock # _____

Make: _____ Model: _____

Repeat/Referral: Y/N _____

NOTES:

_____

_____

_____

_____

_____

_____

_____

_____

_____

_____

_____

_____/20_____

New ☐ CPO ☐ Used ☐   Date ___/___/____

Deal Number: _____ Stock Number: _____

Client's Name: _____/Spouse: _____

Make: _____ Model: _____

Trade Yes/No   Trade Stock # _____

Make: _____ Model: _____

Repeat/Referral: Y/N _____

NOTES:

_____
_____
_____
_____
_____
_____
_____
_____
_____
_____
_____
_____

New ☐ CPO ☐ Used ☐   Date ___/___/___

Deal Number: _____ Stock Number: _____

Client's Name: _____/Spouse: _____

Make: _____ Model: _____

Trade Yes/No   Trade Stock # _____

Make: _____ Model: _____

Repeat/Referral: Y/N _____

NOTES:

_____

_____

_____

_____

_____

_____

_____

_____

_____

_____

_____

_____

_____

_____ /20 _____

New ☐ CPO ☐ Used ☐   Date ___/___/_____

Deal Number: _____ Stock Number: _____

Client's Name: _____/Spouse: _____

Make: _____ Model: _____

Trade Yes/No   Trade Stock # _____

Make: _____ Model: _____

Repeat/Referral: Y/N _____

NOTES:

_____
_____
_____
_____
_____
_____
_____
_____
_____
_____
_____
_____
_____

New ☐ CPO ☐ Used ☐   Date ___/___/___

Deal Number: _____ Stock Number: _____

Client's Name: _____/Spouse: _____

Make: _____ Model: _____

Trade Yes/No   Trade Stock # _____

Make: _____ Model: _____

Repeat/Referral: Y/N _____

NOTES:

_____
_____
_____
_____
_____
_____
_____
_____
_____
_____
_____
_____
_____

_____ /20

New ☐ CPO ☐ Used ☐   Date __/__/____

Deal Number: _____ Stock Number: _____

Client's Name: _____/Spouse: _____

Make: _____ Model: _____

Trade Yes/No   Trade Stock # _____

Make: _____ Model: _____

Repeat/Referral: Y/N _____

NOTES:

_____

_____

_____

_____

_____

_____

_____

_____

_____

_____

_____

_____

_____ /20

New ☐ CPO ☐ Used ☐   Date ___/___/___

Deal Number: _____ Stock Number: _____

Client's Name: _____/Spouse: _____

Make: _____ Model: _____

Trade Yes/No   Trade Stock # _____

Make: _____ Model: _____

Repeat/Referral: Y/N _____

NOTES:

_____

_____

_____

_____

_____

_____

_____

_____

_____

_____

_____

_____

_____

New ☐ CPO ☐ Used ☐   Date ___/___/___

Deal Number: _____ Stock Number: _____

Client's Name: _____/Spouse: _____

Make: _____ Model: _____

Trade Yes/No   Trade Stock # _____

Make: _____ Model: _____

Repeat/Referral: Y/N _____

NOTES:

_____

_____

_____

_____

_____

_____

_____

_____

_____

_____

_____

_____

_____ /20

New ☐ CPO ☐ Used ☐   Date __/__/__

Deal Number: _____ Stock Number: _____

Client's Name: _____/Spouse: _____

Make: _____   Model: _____

Trade Yes/No   Trade Stock # _____

Make: _____   Model: _____

Repeat/Referral: Y/N _____

NOTES:

_____

_____

_____

_____

_____

_____

_____

_____

_____

_____

_____

_____

_____/20

New ☐ CPO ☐ Used ☐   Date ___/___/____

Deal Number: _____ Stock Number: _____

Client's Name: _____/Spouse: _____

Make: _____ Model: _____

Trade Yes/No   Trade Stock # _____

Make: _____ Model: _____

Repeat/Referral: Y/N _____

NOTES:

_____

_____

_____

_____

_____

_____

_____

_____

_____

_____

_____

_____

New ☐ CPO ☐ Used ☐   Date __/__/____

Deal Number: _____ Stock Number: _____

Client's Name: _____/Spouse: _____

Make: _____ Model: _____

Trade Yes/No   Trade Stock # _____

Make: _____ Model: _____

Repeat/Referral: Y/N _____

NOTES:

_____
_____
_____
_____
_____
_____
_____
_____
_____
_____
_____
_____

_____ /20

New ☐ CPO ☐ Used ☐   Date __/__/____

Deal Number: _____ Stock Number: _____

Client's Name: _____/Spouse: _____

Make: _____ Model: _____

Trade Yes/No   Trade Stock # _____

Make: _____ Model: _____

Repeat/Referral: Y/N _____

NOTES:

_____

_____

_____

_____

_____

_____

_____

_____

_____

_____

_____

_____

New ☐ CPO ☐ Used ☐   Date ___/___/___

Deal Number: _____ Stock Number: _____

Client's Name: _____/Spouse: _____

Make: _____ Model: _____

Trade Yes/No   Trade Stock # _____

Make: _____ Model: _____

Repeat/Referral: Y/N _____

NOTES:

_____

_____

_____

_____

_____

_____

_____

_____

_____

_____

_____

_____

New ☐ CPO ☐ Used ☐   Date ___/___/___

Deal Number: _____ Stock Number: _____

Client's Name: _____/Spouse: _____

Make: _____ Model: _____

Trade Yes/No   Trade Stock # _____

Make: _____ Model: _____

Repeat/Referral: Y/N _____

NOTES:

_____
_____
_____
_____
_____
_____
_____
_____
_____
_____
_____
_____
_____

New ☐ CPO ☐ Used ☐   Date __/__/____

Deal Number: _____ Stock Number: _____

Client's Name: _____/Spouse: _____

Make: _____ Model: _____

Trade Yes/No   Trade Stock # _____

Make: _____ Model: _____

Repeat/Referral: Y/N _____

NOTES:

_____
_____
_____
_____
_____
_____
_____
_____
_____
_____
_____

_____ /20

New ☐ CPO ☐ Used ☐   Date __/__/____

Deal Number: _____ Stock Number: _____

Client's Name: _____/Spouse: _____

Make: _____ Model: _____

Trade Yes/No   Trade Stock # _____

Make: _____ Model: _____

Repeat/Referral: Y/N _____

NOTES:

_____

_____

_____

_____

_____

_____

_____

_____

_____

_____

_____

_____

_____/20____

New ☐ CPO ☐ Used ☐   Date ___/___/_____

Deal Number: _____ Stock Number: _____

Client's Name: _____/Spouse: _____

Make: _____ Model: _____

Trade Yes/No   Trade Stock # _____

Make: _____ Model: _____

Repeat/Referral: Y/N _____

NOTES:

_____
_____
_____
_____
_____
_____
_____
_____
_____
_____
_____
_____
_____

_____ /20 _____

New ☐ CPO ☐ Used ☐   Date ___/___/___

Deal Number: _____ Stock Number: _____

Client's Name: _____/Spouse: _____

Make: _____ Model: _____

Trade Yes/No   Trade Stock # _____

Make: _____ Model: _____

Repeat/Referral: Y/N _____

NOTES:

_____

_____

_____

_____

_____

_____

_____

_____

_____

_____

_____

_____

New ☐ CPO ☐ Used ☐   Date ___/___/___

Deal Number: _____ Stock Number: _____

Client's Name: _____/Spouse: _____

Make: _____ Model: _____

Trade Yes/No   Trade Stock # _____

Make: _____ Model: _____

Repeat/Referral: Y/N _____

NOTES:

_____
_____
_____
_____
_____
_____
_____
_____
_____
_____
_____
_____

_____ /20 _____

New ☐ CPO ☐ Used ☐   Date ___/___/___

Deal Number: _____ Stock Number: _____

Client's Name: _____/Spouse: _____

Make: _____ Model: _____

Trade Yes/No   Trade Stock # _____

Make: _____ Model: _____

Repeat/Referral: Y/N _____

NOTES:

_____

_____

_____

_____

_____

_____

_____

_____

_____

_____

_____

_____

_____

_____ /20

New ☐ CPO ☐ Used ☐   Date ___/___/___

Deal Number: _____ Stock Number: _____

Client's Name: _____/Spouse: _____

Make: _____ Model: _____

Trade Yes/No   Trade Stock # _____

Make: _____ Model: _____

Repeat/Referral: Y/N _____

NOTES:

_____

_____

_____

_____

_____

_____

_____

_____

_____

_____

_____

_____

_____ /20

New ☐ CPO ☐ Used ☐   Date ___/___/___

Deal Number: _____ Stock Number: _____

Client's Name: _____/Spouse: _____

Make: _____ Model: _____

Trade Yes/No   Trade Stock # _____

Make: _____ Model: _____

Repeat/Referral: Y/N _____

NOTES:

_____
_____
_____
_____
_____
_____
_____
_____
_____
_____
_____
_____
_____

New ☐ CPO ☐ Used ☐   Date ___/___/___

Deal Number: _____ Stock Number: _____

Client's Name: _____/Spouse: _____

Make: _____ Model: _____

Trade Yes/No   Trade Stock # _____

Make: _____ Model: _____

Repeat/Referral: Y/N _____

NOTES:

_____
_____
_____
_____
_____
_____
_____
_____
_____
_____
_____
_____
_____

New ☐ CPO ☐ Used ☐   Date __/__/____

Deal Number: _____ Stock Number: _____

Client's Name: _____/Spouse: _____

Make: _____ Model: _____

Trade Yes/No   Trade Stock # _____

Make: _____ Model: _____

Repeat/Referral: Y/N _____

NOTES:

_____

_____

_____

_____

_____

_____

_____

_____

_____

_____

_____

_____

_____ /20

New ☐ CPO ☐ Used ☐   Date __/__/__

Deal Number: _____ Stock Number: _____

Client's Name: _____/Spouse: _____

Make: _____ Model: _____

Trade Yes/No   Trade Stock # _____

Make: _____ Model: _____

Repeat/Referral: Y/N _____

NOTES:

_____

_____

_____

_____

_____

_____

_____

_____

_____

_____

_____

_____

_____/20_____

New ☐ CPO ☐ Used ☐   Date __/__/____

Deal Number: _____ Stock Number: _____

Client's Name: _____/Spouse: _____

Make: _____ Model: _____

Trade Yes/No   Trade Stock # _____

Make: _____ Model: _____

Repeat/Referral: Y/N _____

NOTES:

_____

_____

_____

_____

_____

_____

_____

_____

_____

_____

_____

_____

_____ /20

New ☐ CPO ☐ Used ☐   Date ___ / ___ / ___

Deal Number: _____ Stock Number: _____

Client's Name: _____/Spouse: _____

Make: _____ Model: _____

Trade Yes/No   Trade Stock # _____

Make: _____ Model: _____

Repeat/Referral: Y/N _____

NOTES:

_____
_____
_____
_____
_____
_____
_____
_____
_____
_____
_____
_____
_____
_____

_____ /20 _____

New ☐ CPO ☐ Used ☐   Date ___/___/_____

Deal Number: _____ Stock Number: _____ _____

Client's Name: _____/Spouse: _____

Make: _____ Model: _____

Trade Yes/No   Trade Stock # _____

Make: _____ Model: _____

Repeat/Referral: Y/N _____

NOTES:

_____

_____

_____

_____

_____

_____

_____

_____

_____

_____

_____

_____

_____ /20

New ☐ CPO ☐ Used ☐   Date ___/___/___

Deal Number: _____ Stock Number: _____

Client's Name: _____/Spouse: _____

Make: _____ Model: _____

Trade Yes/No   Trade Stock # _____

Make: _____ Model: _____

Repeat/Referral: Y/N _____

NOTES:

_____

_____

_____

_____

_____

_____

_____

_____

_____

_____

_____

New ☐ CPO ☐ Used ☐   Date ___/___/___

Deal Number: _____ Stock Number: _____

Client's Name: _____/Spouse: _____

Make: _____ Model: _____

Trade Yes/No   Trade Stock # _____

Make: _____ Model: _____

Repeat/Referral: Y/N _____

NOTES:

_____
_____
_____
_____
_____
_____
_____
_____
_____
_____
_____
_____
_____

New ☐ CPO ☐ Used ☐   Date __ / __ / ____

Deal Number: _____ Stock Number: _____

Client's Name: _____/Spouse: _____

Make: _____ Model: _____

Trade Yes/No   Trade Stock # _____

Make: _____ Model: _____

Repeat/Referral: Y/N _____

NOTES:

_____

_____

_____

_____

_____

_____

_____

_____

_____

_____

_____

_____

_____/20_____

New ☐ CPO ☐ Used ☐   Date ___/___/___

Deal Number: _____ Stock Number: _____

Client's Name: _____/Spouse: _____

Make: _____ Model: _____

Trade Yes/No   Trade Stock # _____

Make: _____ Model: _____

Repeat/Referral: Y/N _____

NOTES:

_____

_____

_____

_____

_____

_____

_____

_____

_____

_____

_____

_____

New ☐ CPO ☐ Used ☐   Date ___/___/___

Deal Number: _____ Stock Number: _____

Client's Name: _____/Spouse: _____

Make: _____ Model: _____

Trade Yes/No   Trade Stock # _____

Make: _____ Model: _____

Repeat/Referral: Y/N _____

NOTES:

_____

_____

_____

_____

_____

_____

_____

_____

_____

_____

_____

_____

New ☐ CPO ☐ Used ☐   Date ___/___/_____

Deal Number: _____ Stock Number: _____

Client's Name: _____/Spouse: _____

Make: _____ Model: _____

Trade Yes/No   Trade Stock # _____

Make: _____ Model: _____

Repeat/Referral: Y/N _____

NOTES:

_____

_____

_____

_____

_____

_____

_____

_____

_____

_____

_____

_____

New ☐ CPO ☐ Used ☐   Date ___/___/___

Deal Number: _____ Stock Number: _____

Client's Name: _____/Spouse: _____

Make: _____ Model: _____

Trade Yes/No   Trade Stock # _____

Make: _____ Model: _____

Repeat/Referral: Y/N _____

NOTES:

_____

_____

_____

_____

_____

_____

_____

_____

_____

_____

_____

New ☐ CPO ☐ Used ☐   Date ___/___/_____

Deal Number: _____ Stock Number: _____

Client's Name: _____/Spouse: _____

Make: _____ Model: _____

Trade Yes/No   Trade Stock # _____

Make: _____ Model: _____

Repeat/Referral: Y/N _____

NOTES:

_____
_____
_____
_____
_____
_____
_____
_____
_____
_____
_____
_____
_____

New ☐ CPO ☐ Used ☐   Date __/__/____

Deal Number: _____ Stock Number: _____

Client's Name: _____/Spouse: _____

Make: _____ Model: _____

Trade Yes/No   Trade Stock # _____

Make: _____ Model: _____

Repeat/Referral: Y/N _____

NOTES:

_____

_____

_____

_____

_____

_____

_____

_____

_____

_____

_____

_____ /20

New ☐ CPO ☐ Used ☐   Date ___/___/___

Deal Number: _____ Stock Number: _____

Client's Name: _____/Spouse: _____

Make: _____ Model: _____

Trade Yes/No   Trade Stock # _____

Make: _____ Model: _____

Repeat/Referral: Y/N _____

NOTES:

_____

_____

_____

_____

_____

_____

_____

_____

_____

_____

_____

_____

New ☐ CPO ☐ Used ☐   Date ___/___/___

Deal Number: _____ Stock Number: _____

Client's Name: _____/Spouse: _____

Make: _____ Model: _____

Trade Yes/No   Trade Stock # _____

Make: _____ Model: _____

Repeat/Referral: Y/N _____

NOTES:

_____

_____

_____

_____

_____

_____

_____

_____

_____

_____

_____

New ☐ CPO ☐ Used ☐   Date ___/___/___

Deal Number: _____ Stock Number: _____

Client's Name: _____/Spouse: _____

Make: _____ Model: _____

Trade Yes/No   Trade Stock # _____

Make: _____ Model: _____

Repeat/Referral: Y/N _____

NOTES:

_____

_____

_____

_____

_____

_____

_____

_____

_____

_____

_____

New ☐ CPO ☐ Used ☐   Date __/__/___

Deal Number: _____ Stock Number: _____

Client's Name: _____/Spouse: _____

Make: _____ Model: _____

Trade Yes/No   Trade Stock # _____

Make: _____ Model: _____

Repeat/Referral: Y/N _____

NOTES:

_____

_____

_____

_____

_____

_____

_____

_____

_____

_____

_____

_____

_____/20_____

New ☐ CPO ☐ Used ☐   Date ___/___/___

Deal Number: _____ Stock Number: _____

Client's Name: _____/Spouse: _____

Make: _____ Model: _____

Trade Yes/No   Trade Stock # _____

Make: _____ Model: _____

Repeat/Referral: Y/N _____

NOTES:

_____
_____
_____
_____
_____
_____
_____
_____
_____
_____
_____
_____

_____/20_____

New ☐ CPO ☐ Used ☐   Date __/__/____

Deal Number: _____ Stock Number: _____

Client's Name: _____/Spouse: _____

Make: _____ Model: _____

Trade Yes/No   Trade Stock # _____

Make: _____ Model: _____

Repeat/Referral: Y/N _____

NOTES:

_____

_____

_____

_____

_____

_____

_____

_____

_____

_____

_____

_____

_____/20____

New ☐ CPO ☐ Used ☐   Date ___/___/____

Deal Number: _____ Stock Number: _____

Client's Name: _____/Spouse: _____

Make: _____ Model: _____

Trade Yes/No   Trade Stock # _____

Make: _____ Model: _____

Repeat/Referral: Y/N _____

NOTES:

_____

_____

_____

_____

_____

_____

_____

_____

_____

_____

_____

_____

New ☐ CPO ☐ Used ☐   Date ___/___/___

Deal Number: _____ Stock Number: _____

Client's Name: _____/Spouse: _____

Make: _____ Model: _____

Trade Yes/No   Trade Stock # _____

Make: _____ Model: _____

Repeat/Referral: Y/N _____

NOTES:

_____

_____

_____

_____

_____

_____

_____

_____

_____

_____

_____

_____

New ☐ CPO ☐ Used ☐   Date __/__/____

Deal Number: _____ Stock Number: _____

Client's Name: _____/Spouse: _____

Make: _____ Model: _____

Trade Yes/No   Trade Stock # _____

Make: _____ Model: _____

Repeat/Referral: Y/N _____

NOTES:

_____

_____

_____

_____

_____

_____

_____

_____

_____

_____

_____

_____

New ☐ CPO ☐ Used ☐   Date __/__/____

Deal Number: _____ Stock Number: _____

Client's Name: _____/Spouse: _____

Make: _____ Model: _____

Trade Yes/No   Trade Stock # _____

Make: _____ Model: _____

Repeat/Referral: Y/N _____

NOTES:

_____

_____

_____

_____

_____

_____

_____

_____

_____

_____

_____

_____

_____ /20

New ☐ CPO ☐ Used ☐   Date __/__/____

Deal Number: _____ Stock Number: _____

Client's Name: _____/Spouse: _____

Make: _____ Model: _____

Trade Yes/No   Trade Stock # _____

Make: _____ Model: _____

Repeat/Referral: Y/N _____

NOTES:

_____
_____
_____
_____
_____
_____
_____
_____
_____
_____
_____
_____

New ☐ CPO ☐ Used ☐   Date __/__/____

Deal Number: _____ Stock Number: _____

Client's Name: _____/Spouse: _____

Make: _____ Model: _____

Trade Yes/No   Trade Stock # _____

Make: _____ Model: _____

Repeat/Referral: Y/N _____

NOTES:

_____

_____

_____

_____

_____

_____

_____

_____

_____

_____

_____

_____

_____

_____ /20 _____

New ☐ CPO ☐ Used ☐   Date __/__/____

Deal Number: _____ Stock Number: _____

Client's Name: _____/Spouse: _____

Make: _____ Model: _____

Trade Yes/No   Trade Stock # _____

Make: _____ Model: _____

Repeat/Referral: Y/N _____

NOTES:

_____

_____

_____

_____

_____

_____

_____

_____

_____

_____

_____

_____ /20

New ☐ CPO ☐ Used ☐   Date ___/___/___

Deal Number: _____ Stock Number: _____

Client's Name: _____/Spouse: _____

Make: _____   Model: _____

Trade Yes/No   Trade Stock # _____

Make: _____   Model: _____

Repeat/Referral: Y/N _____

NOTES:

_____

_____

_____

_____

_____

_____

_____

_____

_____

_____

_____

_____

New ☐ CPO ☐ Used ☐   Date __/__/____

Deal Number: _____ Stock Number: _____

Client's Name: _____/Spouse: _____

Make: _____ Model: _____

Trade Yes/No   Trade Stock # _____

Make: _____ Model: _____

Repeat/Referral: Y/N _____

NOTES:

_____
_____
_____
_____
_____
_____
_____
_____
_____
_____
_____
_____
_____

_____/20

New ☐ CPO ☐ Used ☐   Date ___/___/___

Deal Number: _____ Stock Number: _____

Client's Name: _____/Spouse: _____

Make: _____ Model: _____

Trade Yes/No   Trade Stock # _____

Make: _____ Model: _____

Repeat/Referral: Y/N _____

NOTES:

_____
_____
_____
_____
_____
_____
_____
_____
_____
_____
_____
_____
_____

_____ /20 _____

New ☐ CPO ☐ Used ☐   Date ___/___/___

Deal Number: _____ Stock Number: _____

Client's Name: _____/Spouse: _____

Make: _____ Model: _____

Trade Yes/No   Trade Stock # _____

Make: _____ Model: _____

Repeat/Referral: Y/N _____

NOTES:

_____
_____
_____
_____
_____
_____
_____
_____
_____
_____
_____
_____
_____
_____

_____ /20

New ☐ CPO ☐ Used ☐   Date ___/___/___

Deal Number: _____ Stock Number: _____

Client's Name: _____/Spouse: _____

Make: _____ Model: _____

Trade Yes/No   Trade Stock # _____

Make: _____ Model: _____

Repeat/Referral: Y/N _____

NOTES:

_____

_____

_____

_____

_____

_____

_____

_____

_____

_____

_____

New ☐ CPO ☐ Used ☐   Date ___/___/___

Deal Number: _____ Stock Number: _____

Client's Name: _____/Spouse: _____

Make: _____ Model: _____

Trade Yes/No   Trade Stock # _____

Make: _____ Model: _____

Repeat/Referral: Y/N _____

NOTES:

_____

_____

_____

_____

_____

_____

_____

_____

_____

_____

_____

_____

New ☐ CPO ☐ Used ☐   Date __/__/____

Deal Number: _____ Stock Number: _____

Client's Name: _____/Spouse: _____

Make: _____ Model: _____

Trade Yes/No   Trade Stock # _____

Make: _____ Model: _____

Repeat/Referral: Y/N _____

NOTES:

_____
_____
_____
_____
_____
_____
_____
_____
_____
_____
_____
_____
_____

_____ /20 _____

New ☐ CPO ☐ Used ☐   Date ___/___/_____

Deal Number: _____ Stock Number: _____ ___

Client's Name: _____/Spouse: _____

Make: _____ Model: _____

Trade Yes/No   Trade Stock # _____

Make: _____ Model: _____

Repeat/Referral: Y/N _____

NOTES:

_____
_____
_____
_____
_____
_____
_____
_____
_____
_____
_____
_____

_____ /20 _____

New ☐ CPO ☐ Used ☐   Date __ / __ / __

Deal Number: _____ Stock Number: _____

Client's Name: _____ /Spouse: _____

Make: _____ Model: _____

Trade Yes/No   Trade Stock # _____

Make: _____ Model: _____

Repeat/Referral: Y/N _____

NOTES:

_____
_____
_____
_____
_____
_____
_____
_____
_____
_____
_____
_____
_____

_____/20

New ☐ CPO ☐ Used ☐   Date ___/___/___

Deal Number: _____ Stock Number: _____

Client's Name: _____/Spouse: _____

Make: _____ Model: _____

Trade Yes/No   Trade Stock # _____

Make: _____ Model: _____

Repeat/Referral: Y/N _____

NOTES:

_____

_____

_____

_____

_____

_____

_____

_____

_____

_____

_____

New ☐ CPO ☐ Used ☐   Date __/__/____

Deal Number: _____ Stock Number: _____

Client's Name: _____/Spouse: _____

Make: _____ Model: _____

Trade Yes/No   Trade Stock # _____

Make: _____ Model: _____

Repeat/Referral: Y/N _____

NOTES:

_____

_____

_____

_____

_____

_____

_____

_____

_____

_____

_____

_____

_____ /20

New ☐ CPO ☐ Used ☐   Date __/__/____

Deal Number: _____ Stock Number: _____

Client's Name: _____/Spouse: _____

Make: _____ Model: _____

Trade Yes/No   Trade Stock # _____

Make: _____ Model: _____

Repeat/Referral: Y/N _____

NOTES:

_____

_____

_____

_____

_____

_____

_____

_____

_____

_____

_____

_____

_____

_____/20_____

New ☐ CPO ☐ Used ☐   Date ___/___/_____

Deal Number: _____ Stock Number: _____

Client's Name: _____/Spouse: _____

Make: _____ Model: _____

Trade Yes/No   Trade Stock # _____

Make: _____ Model: _____

Repeat/Referral: Y/N _____

NOTES:

_____

_____

_____

_____

_____

_____

_____

_____

_____

_____

_____

_____

New ☐ CPO ☐ Used ☐   Date __/__/___

Deal Number: _____ Stock Number: _____

Client's Name: _____/Spouse: _____

Make: _____ Model: _____

Trade Yes/No   Trade Stock # _____

Make: _____ Model: _____

Repeat/Referral: Y/N _____

NOTES:

_____
_____
_____
_____
_____
_____
_____
_____
_____
_____
_____
_____
_____

_____ /20

New ☐ CPO ☐ Used ☐   Date ___/___/___

Deal Number: _____ Stock Number: _____

Client's Name: _____/Spouse: _____

Make: _____ Model: _____

Trade Yes/No   Trade Stock # _____

Make: _____ Model: _____

Repeat/Referral: Y/N _____

NOTES:

_____
_____
_____
_____
_____
_____
_____
_____
_____
_____
_____
_____

_____/20

New ☐ CPO ☐ Used ☐   Date __/__/____

Deal Number: _____ Stock Number: _____

Client's Name: _____/Spouse: _____

Make: _____ Model: _____

Trade Yes/No   Trade Stock # _____

Make: _____ Model: _____

Repeat/Referral: Y/N _____

NOTES:

_____
_____
_____
_____
_____
_____
_____
_____
_____
_____
_____
_____

New ☐ CPO ☐ Used ☐   Date __/__/____

Deal Number: _____ Stock Number: _____

Client's Name: _____/Spouse: _____

Make: _____ Model: _____

Trade Yes/No   Trade Stock # _____

Make: _____ Model: _____

Repeat/Referral: Y/N _____

NOTES:

_____

_____

_____

_____

_____

_____

_____

_____

_____

_____

_____

_____

New ☐ CPO ☐ Used ☐   Date ___/___/___

Deal Number: _____ Stock Number: _____

Client's Name: _____/Spouse: _____

Make: _____ Model: _____

Trade Yes/No   Trade Stock # _____

Make: _____ Model: _____

Repeat/Referral: Y/N _____

NOTES:

_____
_____
_____
_____
_____
_____
_____
_____
_____
_____
_____
_____
_____

_____/20

New ☐ CPO ☐ Used ☐   Date ___/___/___

Deal Number: _____ Stock Number: _____

Client's Name: _____/Spouse: _____

Make: _____ Model: _____

Trade Yes/No   Trade Stock # _____

Make: _____ Model: _____

Repeat/Referral: Y/N _____

NOTES:

_____
_____
_____
_____
_____
_____
_____
_____
_____
_____
_____
_____
_____

_____ /20 _____

New ☐ CPO ☐ Used ☐   Date ___/___/_____

Deal Number: _____ Stock Number: _____

Client's Name: _____/Spouse: _____

Make: _____ Model: _____

Trade Yes/No   Trade Stock # _____

Make: _____ Model: _____

Repeat/Referral: Y/N _____

NOTES:

_____
_____
_____
_____
_____
_____
_____
_____
_____
_____
_____
_____
_____

New ☐ CPO ☐ Used ☐   Date ___/___/___

Deal Number: _____ Stock Number: _____

Client's Name: _____/Spouse: _____

Make: _____ Model: _____

Trade Yes/No   Trade Stock # _____

Make: _____ Model: _____

Repeat/Referral: Y/N _____

NOTES:

_____

_____

_____

_____

_____

_____

_____

_____

_____

_____

_____

_____

_____

_____ /20 _____

New ☐ CPO ☐ Used ☐   Date __/__/____

Deal Number: _____ Stock Number: _____

Client's Name: _____/Spouse: _____

Make: _____ Model: _____

Trade Yes/No   Trade Stock # _____

Make: _____ Model: _____

Repeat/Referral: Y/N _____

NOTES:

_____

_____

_____

_____

_____

_____

_____

_____

_____

_____

_____

New ☐ CPO ☐ Used ☐   Date ___/___/___

Deal Number: _____ Stock Number: _____

Client's Name: _____/Spouse: _____

Make: _____ Model: _____

Trade Yes/No   Trade Stock # _____

Make: _____ Model: _____

Repeat/Referral: Y/N _____

NOTES:

_____

_____

_____

_____

_____

_____

_____

_____

_____

_____

_____

_____

_____

New ☐ CPO ☐ Used ☐   Date ___ / ___ / ___

Deal Number: _____ Stock Number: _____

Client's Name: _____/Spouse: _____

Make: _____ Model: _____

Trade Yes/No   Trade Stock # _____

Make: _____ Model: _____

Repeat/Referral: Y/N _____

NOTES:

_____

_____

_____

_____

_____

_____

_____

_____

_____

_____

_____

_____

_____ /20 _____

New ☐ CPO ☐ Used ☐   Date __/__/____

Deal Number: _____ Stock Number: _____

Client's Name: _____/Spouse: _____

Make: _____ Model: _____

Trade Yes/No   Trade Stock # _____

Make: _____ Model: _____

Repeat/Referral: Y/N _____

NOTES:

_____

_____

_____

_____

_____

_____

_____

_____

_____

_____

_____

_____

New ☐ CPO ☐ Used ☐   Date ___/___/___

Deal Number: _____ Stock Number: _____

Client's Name: _____/Spouse: _____

Make: _____ Model: _____

Trade Yes/No   Trade Stock # _____

Make: _____ Model: _____

Repeat/Referral: Y/N _____

NOTES:

_____
_____
_____
_____
_____
_____
_____
_____
_____
_____
_____
_____

New ☐ CPO ☐ Used ☐   Date ___/___/___

Deal Number: _____ Stock Number: _____

Client's Name: _____/Spouse: _____

Make: _____ Model: _____

Trade Yes/No   Trade Stock # _____

Make: _____ Model: _____

Repeat/Referral: Y/N _____

NOTES:

_____

_____

_____

_____

_____

_____

_____

_____

_____

_____

_____

_____

New ☐ CPO ☐ Used ☐   Date __/__/____

Deal Number: _____ Stock Number: _____

Client's Name: _____/Spouse: _____

Make: _____ Model: _____

Trade Yes/No   Trade Stock # _____

Make: _____ Model: _____

Repeat/Referral: Y/N _____

NOTES:

_____

_____

_____

_____

_____

_____

_____

_____

_____

_____

_____

_____

New ☐ CPO ☐ Used ☐   Date ___/___/___

Deal Number: _____ Stock Number: _____

Client's Name: _____/Spouse: _____

Make: _____ Model: _____

Trade Yes/No   Trade Stock # _____

Make: _____ Model: _____

Repeat/Referral: Y/N _____

NOTES:

_____

_____

_____

_____

_____

_____

_____

_____

_____

_____

_____

_____

_____

New ☐ CPO ☐ Used ☐   Date ___/___/_____

Deal Number: _____ Stock Number: _____

Client's Name: _____/Spouse: _____

Make: _____ Model: _____

Trade Yes/No   Trade Stock # _____

Make: _____ Model: _____

Repeat/Referral: Y/N _____

NOTES:

_____
_____
_____
_____
_____
_____
_____
_____
_____
_____
_____
_____

_____ /20

New ☐ CPO ☐ Used ☐   Date ___/___/_____

Deal Number: _____ Stock Number: _____

Client's Name: _____/Spouse: _____

Make: _____ Model: _____

Trade Yes/No   Trade Stock # _____

Make: _____ Model: _____

Repeat/Referral: Y/N _____

NOTES:

_____
_____
_____
_____
_____
_____
_____
_____
_____
_____
_____
_____

_____/20___

New ☐ CPO ☐ Used ☐   Date ___/___/___

Deal Number: _____ Stock Number: _____

Client's Name: _____/Spouse: _____

Make: _____ Model: _____

Trade Yes/No   Trade Stock # _____

Make: _____ Model: _____

Repeat/Referral: Y/N _____

NOTES:

_____
_____
_____
_____
_____
_____
_____
_____
_____
_____
_____
_____
_____

_____ /20 _____

New ☐ CPO ☐ Used ☐   Date ___/___/___

Deal Number: _____ Stock Number: _____

Client's Name: _____/Spouse: _____

Make: _____ Model: _____

Trade Yes/No   Trade Stock # _____

Make: _____ Model: _____

Repeat/Referral: Y/N _____

NOTES:

_____

_____

_____

_____

_____

_____

_____

_____

_____

_____

_____

_____

_____ /20

New ☐ CPO ☐ Used ☐   Date ___/___/___

Deal Number: _____ Stock Number: _____

Client's Name: _____/Spouse: _____

Make: _____ Model: _____

Trade Yes/No   Trade Stock # _____

Make: _____ Model: _____

Repeat/Referral: Y/N _____

NOTES:

_____
_____
_____
_____
_____
_____
_____
_____
_____
_____
_____

New ☐ CPO ☐ Used ☐   Date __/__/____

Deal Number: _____ Stock Number: _____

Client's Name: _____/Spouse: _____

Make: _____ Model: _____

Trade Yes/No   Trade Stock # _____

Make: _____ Model: _____

Repeat/Referral: Y/N _____

NOTES:

_____
_____
_____
_____
_____
_____
_____
_____
_____
_____
_____
_____

New ☐ CPO ☐ Used ☐   Date __/__/____

Deal Number: _____ Stock Number: _____

Client's Name: _____/Spouse: _____

Make: _____ Model: _____

Trade Yes/No   Trade Stock # _____

Make: _____ Model: _____

Repeat/Referral: Y/N _____

NOTES:

_____

_____

_____

_____

_____

_____

_____

_____

_____

_____

_____

_____

_____ /20 _____

New ☐ CPO ☐ Used ☐   Date ___/___/_____

Deal Number: _____ Stock Number: _____

Client's Name: _____/Spouse: _____

Make: _____ Model: _____

Trade Yes/No   Trade Stock # _____

Make: _____ Model: _____

Repeat/Referral: Y/N _____

NOTES:

_____

_____

_____

_____

_____

_____

_____

_____

_____

_____

_____

_____/20___

New ☐ CPO ☐ Used ☐   Date ___/___/___

Deal Number: _____ Stock Number: _____

Client's Name: _____/Spouse: _____

Make: _____ Model: _____

Trade Yes/No   Trade Stock # _____

Make: _____ Model: _____

Repeat/Referral: Y/N _____

NOTES:

_____

_____

_____

_____

_____

_____

_____

_____

_____

_____

_____

_____

New ☐ CPO ☐ Used ☐   Date ___/___/___

Deal Number: _____ Stock Number: _____

Client's Name: _____/Spouse: _____

Make: _____ Model: _____

Trade Yes/No   Trade Stock # _____

Make: _____ Model: _____

Repeat/Referral: Y/N _____

NOTES:

_____

_____

_____

_____

_____

_____

_____

_____

_____

_____

_____

_____

_____ /20

New ☐ CPO ☐ Used ☐   Date __/__/____

Deal Number: _____ Stock Number: _____

Client's Name: _____/Spouse: _____

Make: _____ Model: _____

Trade Yes/No   Trade Stock # _____

Make: _____ Model: _____

Repeat/Referral: Y/N _____

NOTES:

_____

_____

_____

_____

_____

_____

_____

_____

_____

_____

_____

New ☐ CPO ☐ Used ☐   Date __/__/____

Deal Number: _____ Stock Number: _____

Client's Name: _____/Spouse: _____

Make: _____   Model: _____

Trade Yes/No   Trade Stock # _____

Make: _____   Model: _____

Repeat/Referral: Y/N _____

NOTES:

_____

_____

_____

_____

_____

_____

_____

_____

_____

_____

_____

_____

New ☐ CPO ☐ Used ☐   Date ___ / ___ / ___

Deal Number: _____ Stock Number: _____

Client's Name: _____/Spouse: _____

Make: _____ Model: _____

Trade Yes/No   Trade Stock # _____

Make: _____ Model: _____

Repeat/Referral: Y/N _____

NOTES:

_____

_____

_____

_____

_____

_____

_____

_____

_____

_____

_____

New ☐ CPO ☐ Used ☐   Date ___/___/___

Deal Number: _____ Stock Number: _____

Client's Name: _____/Spouse: _____

Make: _____ Model: _____

Trade Yes/No   Trade Stock # _____

Make: _____ Model: _____

Repeat/Referral: Y/N _____

NOTES:

_____

_____

_____

_____

_____

_____

_____

_____

_____

_____

_____

_____

New ☐ CPO ☐ Used ☐   Date __/__/____

Deal Number: _____ Stock Number: _____

Client's Name: _____/Spouse: _____

Make: _____ Model: _____

Trade Yes/No   Trade Stock # _____

Make: _____ Model: _____

Repeat/Referral: Y/N _____

NOTES:

_____

_____

_____

_____

_____

_____

_____

_____

_____

_____

_____

New ☐ CPO ☐ Used ☐   Date ___/___/___

Deal Number: _____ Stock Number: _____

Client's Name: _____/Spouse: _____

Make: _____ Model: _____

Trade Yes/No   Trade Stock # _____

Make: _____ Model: _____

Repeat/Referral: Y/N _____

NOTES:

_____

_____

_____

_____

_____

_____

_____

_____

_____

_____

_____

_____

_____

New ☐ CPO ☐ Used ☐   Date ___/___/___

Deal Number: _____ Stock Number: _____

Client's Name: _____/Spouse: _____

Make: _____ Model: _____

Trade Yes/No   Trade Stock # _____

Make: _____ Model: _____

Repeat/Referral: Y/N _____

NOTES:

_____

_____

_____

_____

_____

_____

_____

_____

_____

_____

_____

_____

New ☐ CPO ☐ Used ☐   Date ___/___/___

Deal Number: _____ Stock Number: _____

Client's Name: _____/Spouse: _____

Make: _____   Model: _____

Trade Yes/No   Trade Stock # _____

Make: _____   Model: _____

Repeat/Referral: Y/N _____

NOTES:

_____

_____

_____

_____

_____

_____

_____

_____

_____

_____

_____

_____

New ☐ CPO ☐ Used ☐   Date ___/___/_____

Deal Number: _____ Stock Number: _____

Client's Name: _____/Spouse: _____

Make: _____ Model: _____

Trade Yes/No   Trade Stock # _____

Make: _____ Model: _____

Repeat/Referral: Y/N _____

NOTES:

_____
_____
_____
_____
_____
_____
_____
_____
_____
_____
_____
_____

_____/20

New ☐ CPO ☐ Used ☐   Date __/__/____

Deal Number: _____ Stock Number: _____

Client's Name: _____/Spouse: _____

Make: _____ Model: _____

Trade Yes/No   Trade Stock # _____

Make: _____ Model: _____

Repeat/Referral: Y/N _____

NOTES:

_____

_____

_____

_____

_____

_____

_____

_____

_____

_____

_____

_____ /20 _____

New ☐ CPO ☐ Used ☐   Date ___ / ___ / ___

Deal Number: _____ Stock Number: _____

Client's Name: _____/Spouse: _____

Make: _____ Model: _____

Trade Yes/No   Trade Stock # _____

Make: _____ Model: _____

Repeat/Referral: Y/N _____

NOTES:

_____

_____

_____

_____

_____

_____

_____

_____

_____

_____

_____

_____

_____ /20

New ☐ CPO ☐ Used ☐   Date __/__/____

Deal Number: _____ Stock Number: _____

Client's Name: _____/Spouse: _____

Make: _____ Model: _____

Trade Yes/No   Trade Stock # _____

Make: _____ Model: _____

Repeat/Referral: Y/N _____

NOTES:

_____

_____

_____

_____

_____

_____

_____

_____

_____

_____

_____

_____

_____ **/20** _____

New ☐ CPO ☐ Used ☐   Date __ / / __

Deal Number: _____ Stock Number: _____

Client's Name: _____/Spouse: _____

Make: _____ Model: _____

Trade Yes/No   Trade Stock # _____

Make: _____ Model: _____

Repeat/Referral: Y/N _____

NOTES:

_____

_____

_____

_____

_____

_____

_____

_____

_____

_____

_____

New ☐ CPO ☐ Used ☐   Date ___/___/___

Deal Number: _____ Stock Number: _____

Client's Name: _____/Spouse: _____

Make: _____ Model: _____

Trade Yes/No   Trade Stock # _____

Make: _____ Model: _____

Repeat/Referral: Y/N _____

NOTES:

_____

_____

_____

_____

_____

_____

_____

_____

_____

_____

_____

New ☐ CPO ☐ Used ☐   Date ___/___/___

Deal Number: _____ Stock Number: _____

Client's Name: _____/Spouse: _____

Make: _____ Model: _____

Trade Yes/No   Trade Stock # _____

Make: _____ Model: _____

Repeat/Referral: Y/N _____

NOTES:

_____

_____

_____

_____

_____

_____

_____

_____

_____

_____

_____

_____

New ☐ CPO ☐ Used ☐   Date ___ / ___ / ___

Deal Number: _____ Stock Number: _____

Client's Name: _____/Spouse: _____

Make: _____ Model: _____

Trade Yes/No   Trade Stock # _____

Make: _____ Model: _____

Repeat/Referral: Y/N _____

NOTES:

_____

_____

_____

_____

_____

_____

_____

_____

_____

_____

_____/20

New ☐ CPO ☐ Used ☐   Date ___/___/___

Deal Number: _____ Stock Number: _____

Client's Name: _____/Spouse: _____

Make: _____ Model: _____

Trade Yes/No   Trade Stock # _____

Make: _____ Model: _____

Repeat/Referral: Y/N _____

NOTES:

_____

_____

_____

_____

_____

_____

_____

_____

_____

_____

_____

New ☐ CPO ☐ Used ☐　　Date __/__/___

Deal Number: _____ Stock Number: _____

Client's Name: _____/Spouse: _____

Make: _____ Model: _____

Trade Yes/No　　　　Trade Stock # _____

Make: _____ Model: _____

Repeat/Referral: Y/N _____

NOTES:

_____

_____

_____

_____

_____

_____

_____

_____

_____

_____

_____

_____

_____

_____ /20

New ☐ CPO ☐ Used ☐   Date ___/___/_____

Deal Number: _____ Stock Number: _____

Client's Name: _____/Spouse: _____

Make: _____ Model: _____

Trade Yes/No   Trade Stock # _____

Make: _____ Model: _____

Repeat/Referral: Y/N _____

NOTES:

_____
_____
_____
_____
_____
_____
_____
_____
_____
_____
_____
_____
_____
_____

_____ /20 _____

New ☐ CPO ☐ Used ☐   Date ___/___/_____

Deal Number: _____ Stock Number: _____

Client's Name: _____/Spouse: _____

Make: _____ Model: _____

Trade Yes/No   Trade Stock # _____

Make: _____ Model: _____

Repeat/Referral: Y/N _____

NOTES:

_____

_____

_____

_____

_____

_____

_____

_____

_____

_____

_____

New ☐ CPO ☐ Used ☐   Date __/__/__

Deal Number: _____ Stock Number: _____

Client's Name: _____/Spouse: _____

Make: _____ Model: _____

Trade Yes/No   Trade Stock # _____

Make: _____ Model: _____

Repeat/Referral: Y/N _____

NOTES:

_____

_____

_____

_____

_____

_____

_____

_____

_____

_____

_____

_____ /20 _____

New ☐ CPO ☐ Used ☐   Date ___/___/_____

Deal Number: _____ Stock Number: _____

Client's Name: _____/Spouse: _____

Make: _____ Model: _____

Trade Yes/No   Trade Stock # _____

Make: _____ Model: _____

Repeat/Referral: Y/N _____

NOTES:

_____

_____

_____

_____

_____

_____

_____

_____

_____

_____

_____

New ☐ CPO ☐ Used ☐   Date ___/___/___

Deal Number: _____ Stock Number: _____

Client's Name: _____/Spouse: _____

Make: _____ Model: _____

Trade Yes/No   Trade Stock # _____

Make: _____ Model: _____

Repeat/Referral: Y/N _____

NOTES:

_____
_____
_____
_____
_____
_____
_____
_____
_____
_____
_____
_____

New ☐ CPO ☐ Used ☐   Date ___/___/___

Deal Number: _____ Stock Number: _____

Client's Name: _____/Spouse: _____

Make: _____ Model: _____

Trade Yes/No   Trade Stock # _____

Make: _____ Model: _____

Repeat/Referral: Y/N _____

NOTES:

_____

_____

_____

_____

_____

_____

_____

_____

_____

_____

_____

_____

_____/20

New ☐ CPO ☐ Used ☐   Date ___/___/___

Deal Number: _____ Stock Number: _____

Client's Name: _____/Spouse: _____

Make: _____ Model: _____

Trade Yes/No   Trade Stock # _____

Make: _____ Model: _____

Repeat/Referral: Y/N _____

NOTES:

_____
_____
_____
_____
_____
_____
_____
_____
_____
_____
_____

New ☐ CPO ☐ Used ☐   Date ___/___/_____

Deal Number: _____ Stock Number: _____

Client's Name: _____/Spouse: _____

Make: _____ Model: _____

Trade Yes/No   Trade Stock # _____

Make: _____ Model: _____

Repeat/Referral: Y/N _____

NOTES:

_____

_____

_____

_____

_____

_____

_____

_____

_____

_____

_____

_____

New ☐ CPO ☐ Used ☐   Date __/__/____

Deal Number: _____ Stock Number: _____

Client's Name: _____/Spouse: _____

Make: _____ Model: _____

Trade Yes/No   Trade Stock # _____

Make: _____ Model: _____

Repeat/Referral: Y/N _____

NOTES:

_____
_____
_____
_____
_____
_____
_____
_____
_____
_____
_____
_____

New ☐ CPO ☐ Used ☐   Date ___/___/_____

Deal Number: _____ Stock Number: _____

Client's Name: _____/Spouse: _____

Make: _____ Model: _____

Trade Yes/No   Trade Stock # _____

Make: _____ Model: _____

Repeat/Referral: Y/N _____

NOTES:

_____
_____
_____
_____
_____
_____
_____
_____
_____
_____
_____
_____

New ☐ CPO ☐ Used ☐   Date ___/___/___

Deal Number: _____ Stock Number: _____

Client's Name: _____/Spouse: _____

Make: _____ Model: _____

Trade Yes/No   Trade Stock # _____

Make: _____ Model: _____

Repeat/Referral: Y/N _____

NOTES:

_____

_____

_____

_____

_____

_____

_____

_____

_____

_____

_____

New ☐ CPO ☐ Used ☐   Date __/__/____

Deal Number: _____ Stock Number: _____

Client's Name: _____/Spouse: _____

Make: _____ Model: _____

Trade Yes/No   Trade Stock # _____

Make: _____ Model: _____

Repeat/Referral: Y/N _____

NOTES:

_____
_____
_____
_____
_____
_____
_____
_____
_____
_____
_____
_____

New ☐ CPO ☐ Used ☐   Date ___ / ___ / ___

Deal Number: _____ Stock Number: _____

Client's Name: _____/Spouse: _____

Make: _____ Model: _____

Trade Yes/No   Trade Stock # _____

Make: _____ Model: _____

Repeat/Referral: Y/N _____

NOTES:

_____

_____

_____

_____

_____

_____

_____

_____

_____

_____

_____

_____

New ☐ CPO ☐ Used ☐   Date __/__/____

Deal Number: _____ Stock Number: _____

Client's Name: _____/Spouse: _____

Make: _____ Model: _____

Trade Yes/No   Trade Stock # _____

Make: _____ Model: _____

Repeat/Referral: Y/N _____

NOTES:

_____

_____

_____

_____

_____

_____

_____

_____

_____

_____

_____

_____/20_____

New ☐ CPO ☐ Used ☐   Date ___/___/_____

Deal Number: _____ Stock Number: _____

Client's Name: _____/Spouse: _____

Make: _____ Model: _____

Trade Yes/No   Trade Stock # _____

Make: _____ Model: _____

Repeat/Referral: Y/N _____

NOTES:

_____

_____

_____

_____

_____

_____

_____

_____

_____

_____

_____

_____

New ☐ CPO ☐ Used ☐   Date ___/___/___

Deal Number: _____ Stock Number: _____

Client's Name: _____/Spouse: _____

Make: _____ Model: _____

Trade Yes/No   Trade Stock # _____

Make: _____ Model: _____

Repeat/Referral: Y/N _____

NOTES:

_____

_____

_____

_____

_____

_____

_____

_____

_____

_____

_____

_____

_____ /20 _____

New ☐ CPO ☐ Used ☐   Date ___/___/___

Deal Number: _____ Stock Number: _____

Client's Name: _____/Spouse: _____

Make: _____ Model: _____

Trade Yes/No   Trade Stock # _____

Make: _____ Model: _____

Repeat/Referral: Y/N _____

NOTES:

_____
_____
_____
_____
_____
_____
_____
_____
_____
_____
_____
_____

New ☐ CPO ☐ Used ☐   Date __/__/____

Deal Number: _____ Stock Number: _____

Client's Name: _____/Spouse: _____

Make: _____ Model: _____

Trade Yes/No   Trade Stock # _____

Make: _____ Model: _____

Repeat/Referral: Y/N _____

NOTES:

_____

_____

_____

_____

_____

_____

_____

_____

_____

_____

_____

_____

New ☐ CPO ☐ Used ☐   Date ___/___/_____

Deal Number: _____ Stock Number: _____

Client's Name: _____/Spouse: _____

Make: _____ Model: _____

Trade Yes/No   Trade Stock # _____

Make: _____ Model: _____

Repeat/Referral: Y/N _____

NOTES:

_____

_____

_____

_____

_____

_____

_____

_____

_____

_____

_____

_____/20

New ☐ CPO ☐ Used ☐   Date ___/___/___

Deal Number: _____ Stock Number: _____

Client's Name: _____/Spouse: _____

Make: _____ Model: _____

Trade Yes/No   Trade Stock # _____

Make: _____ Model: _____

Repeat/Referral: Y/N _____

NOTES:

_____

_____

_____

_____

_____

_____

_____

_____

_____

_____

_____

_____

_____ /20

New ☐ CPO ☐ Used ☐   Date ___/___/___

Deal Number: _____ Stock Number: _____

Client's Name: _____/Spouse: _____

Make: _____ Model: _____

Trade Yes/No   Trade Stock # _____

Make: _____ Model: _____

Repeat/Referral: Y/N _____

NOTES:

_____

_____

_____

_____

_____

_____

_____

_____

_____

_____

_____

_____

New ☐ CPO ☐ Used ☐   Date ___/___/___

Deal Number: _____ Stock Number: _____

Client's Name: _____/Spouse: _____

Make: _____ Model: _____

Trade Yes/No   Trade Stock # _____

Make: _____ Model: _____

Repeat/Referral: Y/N _____

NOTES:

_____

_____

_____

_____

_____

_____

_____

_____

_____

_____

_____

New ☐ CPO ☐ Used ☐   Date __/__/____

Deal Number: _____ Stock Number: _____

Client's Name: _____/Spouse: _____

Make: _____ Model: _____

Trade Yes/No   Trade Stock # _____

Make: _____ Model: _____

Repeat/Referral: Y/N _____

NOTES:

_____
_____
_____
_____
_____
_____
_____
_____
_____
_____
_____

New ☐ CPO ☐ Used ☐   Date ___/___/___

Deal Number: _____ Stock Number: _____

Client's Name: _____/Spouse: _____

Make: _____ Model: _____

Trade Yes/No   Trade Stock # _____

Make: _____ Model: _____

Repeat/Referral: Y/N _____

NOTES:

_____
_____
_____
_____
_____
_____
_____
_____
_____
_____
_____
_____

New ☐ CPO ☐ Used ☐   Date ___/___/___

Deal Number: _____ Stock Number: _____

Client's Name: _____/Spouse: _____

Make: _____ Model: _____

Trade Yes/No   Trade Stock # _____

Make: _____ Model: _____

Repeat/Referral: Y/N _____

NOTES:

_____
_____
_____
_____
_____
_____
_____
_____
_____
_____
_____
_____
_____

_____/20_____

New ☐ CPO ☐ Used ☐   Date ___/___/_____

Deal Number: _____ Stock Number: _____

Client's Name: _____/Spouse: _____

Make: _____ Model: _____

Trade Yes/No   Trade Stock # _____

Make: _____ Model: _____

Repeat/Referral: Y/N _____

NOTES:

_____

_____

_____

_____

_____

_____

_____

_____

_____

_____

_____

_____ /20

New ☐ CPO ☐ Used ☐   Date ___/___/___

Deal Number: _____ Stock Number: _____

Client's Name: _____/Spouse: _____

Make: _____ Model: _____

Trade Yes/No   Trade Stock # _____

Make: _____ Model: _____

Repeat/Referral: Y/N _____

NOTES:

_____

_____

_____

_____

_____

_____

_____

_____

_____

_____

_____

_____

New ☐ CPO ☐ Used ☐   Date __/__/__

Deal Number: _____ Stock Number: _____

Client's Name: _____/Spouse: _____

Make: _____ Model: _____

Trade Yes/No   Trade Stock # _____

Make: _____ Model: _____

Repeat/Referral: Y/N _____

NOTES:

_____

_____

_____

_____

_____

_____

_____

_____

_____

_____

_____

_____

New ☐ CPO ☐ Used ☐   Date ___/___/___

Deal Number: _____ Stock Number: _____

Client's Name: _____/Spouse: _____

Make: _____ Model: _____

Trade Yes/No   Trade Stock # _____

Make: _____ Model: _____

Repeat/Referral: Y/N _____

NOTES:

_____
_____
_____
_____
_____
_____
_____
_____
_____
_____
_____
_____
_____
_____

New ☐ CPO ☐ Used ☐   Date ___/___/___

Deal Number: _____ Stock Number: _____

Client's Name: _____/Spouse: _____

Make: _____ Model: _____

Trade Yes/No   Trade Stock # _____

Make: _____ Model: _____

Repeat/Referral: Y/N _____

NOTES:

_____

_____

_____

_____

_____

_____

_____

_____

_____

_____

_____

_____ /20

New ☐ CPO ☐ Used ☐   Date ___/___/___

Deal Number: _____ Stock Number: _____

Client's Name: _____/Spouse: _____

Make: _____ Model: _____

Trade Yes/No   Trade Stock # _____

Make: _____ Model: _____

Repeat/Referral: Y/N _____

NOTES:

_____
_____
_____
_____
_____
_____
_____
_____
_____
_____
_____
_____

_____ /20

New ☐ CPO ☐ Used ☐   Date ___/___/___

Deal Number: _____ Stock Number: _____

Client's Name: _____/Spouse: _____

Make: _____ Model: _____

Trade Yes/No   Trade Stock # _____

Make: _____ Model: _____

Repeat/Referral: Y/N _____

NOTES:

_____

_____

_____

_____

_____

_____

_____

_____

_____

_____

_____

_____

New ☐ CPO ☐ Used ☐   Date __/__/__

Deal Number: _____ Stock Number: _____

Client's Name: _____/Spouse: _____

Make: _____ Model: _____

Trade Yes/No   Trade Stock # _____

Make: _____ Model: _____

Repeat/Referral: Y/N _____

NOTES:

_____
_____
_____
_____
_____
_____
_____
_____
_____
_____
_____
_____

New ☐ CPO ☐ Used ☐   Date ___/___/___

Deal Number: _____ Stock Number: _____

Client's Name: _____/Spouse: _____

Make: _____ Model: _____

Trade Yes/No   Trade Stock # _____

Make: _____ Model: _____

Repeat/Referral: Y/N _____

NOTES:

_____

_____

_____

_____

_____

_____

_____

_____

_____

_____

_____

_____/20___

New ☐ CPO ☐ Used ☐   Date ___/___/___

Deal Number: _____ Stock Number: _____

Client's Name: _____/Spouse: _____

Make: _____ Model: _____

Trade Yes/No   Trade Stock # _____

Make: _____ Model: _____

Repeat/Referral: Y/N _____

NOTES:

_____

_____

_____

_____

_____

_____

_____

_____

_____

_____

_____

_____

New ☐ CPO ☐ Used ☐   Date ___/___/___

Deal Number: _____ Stock Number: _____

Client's Name: _____/Spouse: _____

Make: _____ Model: _____

Trade Yes/No   Trade Stock # _____

Make: _____ Model: _____

Repeat/Referral: Y/N _____

NOTES:

_____

_____

_____

_____

_____

_____

_____

_____

_____

_____

_____

New ☐ CPO ☐ Used ☐   Date ___/___/___

Deal Number: _____ Stock Number: _____

Client's Name: _____/Spouse: _____

Make: _____ Model: _____

Trade Yes/No   Trade Stock # _____

Make: _____ Model: _____

Repeat/Referral: Y/N _____

NOTES:

_____

_____

_____

_____

_____

_____

_____

_____

_____

_____

_____

_____

New ☐ CPO ☐ Used ☐   Date ___/___/_____

Deal Number: _____ Stock Number: _____

Client's Name: _____/Spouse: _____

Make: _____ Model: _____

Trade Yes/No   Trade Stock # _____

Make: _____ Model: _____

Repeat/Referral: Y/N _____

NOTES:

_____

_____

_____

_____

_____

_____

_____

_____

_____

_____

_____

_____

_____

New ☐ CPO ☐ Used ☐   Date ___/___/___

Deal Number: _____ Stock Number: _____

Client's Name: _____/Spouse: _____

Make: _____ Model: _____

Trade Yes/No   Trade Stock # _____

Make: _____ Model: _____

Repeat/Referral: Y/N _____

NOTES:

_____

_____

_____

_____

_____

_____

_____

_____

_____

_____

_____

***

The Auto Sales Logbook and affiliates are not responsible or liable for any information collected, used, misused, or distributed legally or illegally. The purchaser, owner, or user assumes all responsibility related to The Auto Sales Logbook and the contents inside. Do not collect, store, or distribute information not previously approved by your employer.

***

NOTES

NOTES

NOTES

NOTES

NOTES

_____

_____

_____

_____

_____

_____

_____

_____

_____

_____

_____

_____

_____

_____

NOTES

NOTES

NOTES

To order replacement copies,
scan this QR code to purchase

Made in the USA
Monee, IL
12 December 2024

73413085R00136